I Want to Teach my CHiLD About Money

BY

KATHIE AND DOUG RECHKEMMER

Standard

I Want to Teach My Child About Money
© 2005 Standard Publishing, Cincinnati,
Ohio. A division of Standex International
Corporation. All rights reserved. Printed
in China.

Produced by Susan Lingo Books™
Cover and interior by Diana Walters

12 11 10 09 08 07 06 05   9 8 7 6 5 4 3 2 1
0-7847-1762-1

Contents

Introduction

Why teach your child about money?

Did your parents ever take time to teach you about money management? If they didn't, you probably wish they had—there are so many things to consider and learn when dealing with money! Many children find themselves all grown up and without any real knowledge of money management. They find themselves as adults with little or no understanding of how to save or invest their money—even though there's no problem spending it! Most parents recognize the importance of teaching their children about the "birds and the bees," and most realize why teaching their children to say please and thank you is a necessity. Teaching your child about money concepts is no different. Kids need to learn, develop, and apply money skills that will serve them richly throughout their lifetimes.

I Want to Teach My Child About Money provides heaps of help in teaching your child important concepts such as what money is, how we get and use money, the importance of saving money for the future, and how God desires us to use money. Everything from earning an allowance to tithing and spending responsibly is covered. *I Want to Teach My Child About Money* also equips you with great tips, informative sidebars and boxes, and loads of hands-on ideas to share with your child.

Teaching your child about money and about how God directs us to wisely use and save it will help him today and for his financial lifetime! Help turn your child into a good, financially responsible steward who uses money to serve God and others and to provide for his own security!

Where Do You Stand?

Working toward helping your child learn about money and how it affects her life is an important part of parenting. The following questionnaire will help you evaluate your own strengths and weaknesses and where your own values and philosophies fit in. Circle the box with the number that best corresponds to your answer. Then add up the total of your answers and check out the How You Scored box! (Retake the quiz after reading the book to see if your score changed!)

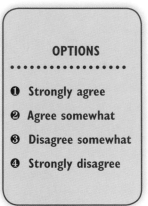

OPTIONS

❶ **Strongly agree**

❷ **Agree somewhat**

❸ **Disagree somewhat**

❹ **Strongly disagree**

I UNDERSTAND MONEY HAS NO VALUE BY ITSELF; IT'S SIMPLY ANOTHER MEANS OF TRADING.

❶   ❷   ❸   ❹

I SET ASIDE TIME TO TALK ABOUT MONEY AND HOW WE USE IT WITH MY CHILD.

❶   ❷   ❸   ❹

I VIEW MONEY AS SIMPLY A TOOL TO HELP ME ACHIEVE GOALS.

❶   ❷   ❸   ❹

I'VE DEVELOPED A BUDGET, HAVE WRITTEN IT ON PAPER, AND STICK TO IT FAITHFULLY.

❶   ❷   ❸   ❹

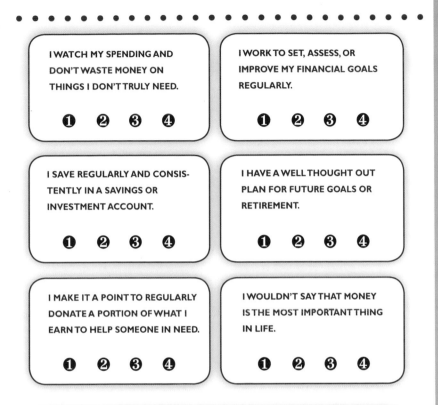

I WATCH MY SPENDING AND DON'T WASTE MONEY ON THINGS I DON'T TRULY NEED.

❶ ❷ ❸ ❹

I WORK TO SET, ASSESS, OR IMPROVE MY FINANCIAL GOALS REGULARLY.

❶ ❷ ❸ ❹

I SAVE REGULARLY AND CONSISTENTLY IN A SAVINGS OR INVESTMENT ACCOUNT.

❶ ❷ ❸ ❹

I HAVE A WELL THOUGHT OUT PLAN FOR FUTURE GOALS OR RETIREMENT.

❶ ❷ ❸ ❹

I MAKE IT A POINT TO REGULARLY DONATE A PORTION OF WHAT I EARN TO HELP SOMEONE IN NEED.

❶ ❷ ❸ ❹

I WOULDN'T SAY THAT MONEY IS THE MOST IMPORTANT THING IN LIFE.

❶ ❷ ❸ ❹

HOW YOU SCORED

10—20 Give yourself a pat on the back! You're able to plan ahead, commit to your goals, and move ahead without overspending or undersaving. The habits you've worked so hard to adopt are the ones you want to instill in your child and will serve him well throughout his life!

21—31 Your money skills might need polishing to really shine! You're a moderate spender—but also a moderate saver. Though you probably have a budget, it may not be written down or stuck to like glue. Help your child realize that careful spending and saving are important all the time.

32—40 Money may travel a little too quickly through your fingers! Though you probably realize money doesn't hold all of life's answers, you tend to see it as a way of getting what you want immediately instead of waiting until you can afford it. With a little budget control and a bit of willpower, you'll be back on the path to healthy money management.

What Is Money?

Children grow up understanding that their parents use coins and paper money, credit cards, or checks to pay for things that they need or want. It is important to teach children about the various forms of money so they can begin to develop an understanding of the value of money.

Money is a means of exchange.

Kids understand the concept of trading between friends and siblings. It's a natural idea, then, for kids to realize that our monetary system began with people trading common items such as shells, animals, and pelts. But as people discovered that trading didn't always work, money became common around the world.

Money replaces bartering.

Our earliest ancestors provided their own food, clothing, and shelter from their surroundings. As larger tribes or communities formed, hunting and gathering became more efficient. If one tribe had more grain than they needed, they could it for another tribe's pelts. This was called bartering and was the first means of exchanging items for what was wanted or needed.

key point
TRADING CREATES DIFFERING VALUES.

key point
BARTERING IS A MEANS OF EXCHANGE.

Bartering wasn't always easy or handy. Just think how difficult it would have been to carry around heavy pelts or skins containing grain! Bartering only worked if one person or tribe had exactly what another wanted and was willing to trade for. And bartering depended on what was considered "valuable." Would you trade a coat for a car?

For kids truly to understand the concept of trade or barter and how it was the first means of exchange, have a little fun letting your kids experiment with their own bartering system around home. Invite everyone in the family to barter or trade for what they need or want during the next few days. If your child wants to watch an hour of television, he might trade that hour for doing the dishes or raking the yard—or even breakfast in bed! Discuss how bartering worked and if the trading was fair. Then trade hugs to help kids learn the value of bartering—and family fun!

BIG BIBLE POINT

" 'Then bring your livestock,' said Joseph, 'I will sell you food in exchange for your livestock, since your money is gone' " (Genesis 47:16). Trading or bartering was used throughout Bible times. Read this verse with your child, then ask:

- Why was bartering a good way of getting what was needed?

- Do you think trading was always fair? Explain.

- How did Jesus "trade" His forgiveness for our sins?

Bartering took the place of money in early times but is still used today.

Money is common all over the world.

In Sumer, one thousand years before Abraham lived, shell coins were used as money. Gold, silver, and copper were used to pay for goods and services as early as 2,500 B.C. in Egypt and Asia. By 700 B.C. coins were pressed with patterns and made of "electrum," a pale yellow alloy of gold and silver. These coins were valuable, strong, and easy to carry instead of hoisting heavy pelts.

key point

MONEY IS USED THE WORLD OVER.

key point

MONEY HAS CHANGED OVER TIME.

TIPS FOR 'TWEENS
Purchase a "50 States Quarters" collectors book from a coin shop or draw a map of the United States on poster board, then tape or glue quarters to the corresponding states.

Kids love discovering interesting tidbits about the history of coins, currencies, and paper money. The concept of paper money can be found in receipts recorded as early as 2,500 B.C. in Babylonia, and the earliest bills may be traced back to China, when Kubla Khan issued paper notes in 1273 made of mulberry bark. In 1690 the Massachusetts Bay Colony issued the first paper money in the thirteen colonies. It wasn't until 1929 that the United States put portraits of past presidents on the faces of the bills and emblems and monuments on the backs.

BIG BIBLE POINT

The earliest use of money in the Bible tells us about gold and is found in Genesis 2:11, 12. **Read this verse and point out that even Adam and Eve could have found gold—about four thousand years before the time of Jesus! Then read the following verses about money and discuss how money was used in each and what we can learn about money.**
• *Genesis 47:15, 16*
• *Exodus 22:25*

You may wish to check out www.usmint.gov to discover more interesting facts about money and the State Quarters Program. Many books at your local library contain fascinating facts about money. Plan a family trip to a coin shop to see how world currencies are similar yet different. Finally, consider starting your own coin collection as a family and decorating a special box in which to keep your treasures!

Use kids' natural curiosity about coins and currencies to remind them that money is a means of exchange the world over! There's even a fancy term for coin collecting: numismatics. Invite kids to compare and contrast the different state quarters they may have. Can you figure out why each state picked the designs used to symbolize that state?

Collecting coins is a great family learning activity!

TIPS FOR TODDLERS

Count with coins and an old calendar! Stick double-sided tape to the backs of small paper "coins." Look at the date boxes on an old calendar and stick the corresponding number of "coins" to the calendar squares. Count with preschoolers. Have older kids use combinations of coins (a nickel plus a dime equals 15).

Money can be an indicator of value.

Money doesn't have any value of its own. It's important for kids to realize that money is simply a tool to help them accomplish goals for their needs and wants.

Money has no "real" value of its own.

Although gold is used most often in jewelry and embellishments, it's also known for its use as money. The phrase "gold standard" means using gold as the standard value for the money in a country. For many years in the United States, every ounce of gold represented one dollar in circulation. Most of the gold in the United States has been kept in a place called Fort Knox.

TIPS FOR TODDLERS

Even very young children can have fun trading and learning that money is used as exchange for something wanted. Cut colored paper into pairs of circles and tape half the circles to toys. Hand the other circles to your child. Explain that a red circle can be traded for a toy with a red circle and so on. Let your child "spend" until he has traded all his paper coins away.

In 1971, President Nixon closed the "gold window," which broke the last ties between the amount of gold and the number of circulating dollars. Paper money was put into common circulation. A dollar used to buy several gallons of gasoline in the 1960s, yet today doesn't buy even one gallon. The value of a dollar keeps changing and is only worth what it can buy at any given time.

TARGET MOMENT

The phrase "In God We Trust" does not appear in the Bible in those exact words, but the United States officially recognized God as the divine protector of its money through the agency of the U.S. Mint. Check your coins to find the words "In God We Trust" and where they appear on each coin or bill.

Most money has no value except as a medium of exchange—in other words, trading for an item or service that a group of people agree has a certain worth. We spend or use dollars to buy what we desire or see as valuable. The dollar has no other use except as a medium of exchange. If people decided that currency was worthless, money wouldn't be worth a penny!

TIPS FOR 'TWEENS

Make "funny money" by cutting out paper dollars and letting your child decide what his money would look like. Use markers to embellish the bills. Then glue a photo of your child's face to the paper bills for personalized money!

Cut a sheet of paper into several pieces and scatter them around the house. After a few hours, assign random value to the papers, such as "one paper equals one dessert of choice." Although kids may have ignored those papers, they will suddenly have great "value"! Discuss how this is like money, which has no value of its own until people assign value to it.

We decide what is valuable to us.

What would life be like without money? How would we pay for food, shelter, clothing, and the other things we need to survive? Without money, we probably wouldn't survive very healthily—or very happily! Money isn't everything, though. We don't need money to play at the park or build a snowman when it snows. And we don't need money to have friends or fun or to show our love for God.

"PRICE IS WHAT YOU PAY. VALUE IS WHAT YOU GET."
—Warren Buffett

Think for a moment about what's valuable in your own life. Maybe you find extraordinary value in your health and family. Matthew 6:21 says, "For where your treasure is, there your heart will be also." Although we value things differently, we all pretty much agree that placing the most worth on treasures of the heart is where the great-est value lies. Money doesn't always mean wealth, worth, or happiness!

PARENTS POINTER

Make a list of things that you can do as a family that are free of cost but fun, too. Suggestions might include a "walk-n-talk" around the block, best-of-the-fall leaf-collecting contest, or even riding free shuttles at the airport. Remind your kids that sometimes the best things in life are free—especially when they are shared with the ones you love!

key point
WE ASSIGN VALUES TO ITEMS.

Which is more valuable to you: an old pair of sneakers or a new vacuum cleaner? Most would probably choose the vacuum to keep their homes clean, right? But if you walked barefooted on thorns, the sneakers would be far more valuable! We assign personal value to goods and services based on how much we need or want something, what others think of the item, and how much in demand that item or service really is.

VALUE IS OFTEN DEFINED BY OUR NEEDS.

key point
ASSIGNED VALUES CHANGE OVER TIME.

Is money the most valuable thing to have? Ask your child to imagine that he is on a deserted island when a suitcase of money washes up on the beach along with a suitcase of assorted foods. Discuss which suitcase your child would rather have and why. Then use old magazines to create a "most valued" collage of pictures that represent treasures in his life.

TIPS FOR 'TWEENS
Give your older child a dollar and turn her loose in a discount store. Challenge your child to purchase as many items as possible with the money. Then discuss how the prices of items may not equal their value! Does one pack of gum really equal the real or perceived value of five pencils?

People assign worth to money.

How important is money to you? Is it more important than love? Is it more important than food? Is it more important than spiritual happiness? The point is, you assign worth and importance to money—and your children learn these same values from you!

Money has purchasing power.

When we have money, we have purchasing power. We're able to buy the things we need and many of the things we want. We have the power to make money and the power to decide how to use our money. But as with any power, there comes responsibility. Kids need to learn early that the power of money can be as quickly lost as it is gained!

TRY THIS!

Write spending or savings goals on colorful index cards, then hang them in a place where they will be seen often. Sometimes just a visual reminder helps us make better choices and attain our goals!

Everyone has a limited amount of money, and how that money is used can mean the difference between being comfortable and secure and being destitute and needy. When we spend too much, our financial freedom is gone. Regardless of the amount of money each of us has, we all have the power to waste it or use it wisely—and this is the most important power of all!

Money does have the power to help us reach good goals for our lives and the power to destroy security and throw us into debt. So how can we control this power to make or break us? And how can we encourage our children to respect the dangerous aspects of money as well as celebrate the positive power of finances? By making savings goals and spending plans!

key point
MONEY CREATES POWER.

Take a moment to consider ...

- *Do you recognize your power over money choices?*

- *What are your spending and savings goals?*

- *What are you doing to reach your goals?*

- *How do your goals reflect your attitudes toward money?*

Have you ever noticed how some people just can't wait to spend the money that they've made or even inherited? Before they know it, their security is gone and they wonder, "Where did it all go? What happened?" Chances are pretty good that no spending plan was ever made—or even considered! Responsibility regarding the power of money begins with wishes, goals, and plans. Goals may start out as simple wishes, and spending or saving plans help to achieve goals.

As a family, choose one or two wishes or goals, then devise a plan to achieve them. Goals may be a trip to a theme park or simply going out to dinner. Work as a family to reach your goal by saving more or spending less!

Vacations are a goal the whole family can save for—and enjoy!

Money rewards our work.

Does your child know what you do for a living? Does she know what kind of schooling you completed or how much money you make? It's important for kids to realize that not all jobs require the same amount of work or are monetarily rewarded the same. Make a list of jobs or professions with your child. Suggestions might include doctor, banker, teacher, lawyer, artist, pet groomer, farmer, veterinarian, musician, and architect. Discuss which jobs require extra training and why. Explain that jobs requiring more training are usually rewarded with more money.

key point

MONEY ISN'T THE ONLY REWARD FOR WORK.

It's helpful to discuss work and your feelings surrounding it with your child. Encourage your child to ask you or other adults about their kinds of work or professions and what rewards they have from their jobs. Encourage your child to find out about the kinds of skills people need for different jobs. Point out that money does reward our time and work, but if someone doesn't enjoy his work, the money may not be enough. Guide your child to realize that, although money is a reward for hard work, there are other rewards as well.

What careers are your kids interested in? For ideas, check out www.bls.gov/k12/.

The older children get, the more ideas they have of what kinds of jobs sound interesting—of course, wait five minutes and plans may change! Kids understand that work takes time and effort and that there are many rewards to jobs done well, including a feeling of accomplishment, pride in doing fine work, and, of course, a bit of money in the pocket or piggy bank! In the real world, money does reward good work.

key point
WORK BRINGS MANY REWARDS.

Job	Recommended Training/Schooling	Average Annual Salary
Minister	4 years or less of training or college	$36,000
Firefighter	2 years of college studying fire science	$36,000
Pilot	4 years of college and flight experience	$47,000
Teacher	4–5 years of college and student teaching	$44,000
Doctor	4 years of college, 4+ years of medical school	$70,000

Money is a useful tool.

There are many ways that money can be useful and help us achieve our wishes and goals. It can help build up the world around us or can be destructive to our personal financial freedom and security. How will you teach your child to use money?

We can put money to work for us.

In Jesus' story of the Ten Talents (Matthew 25:14-30), three men were given "talents" or money in differing amounts. After a time, the man given the most had doubled his money, as well as the man given two talents. But the man given one talent buried his money and still had only one talent to show. As punishment, his talent was taken away. What's the lesson here? *We can choose to use our money wisely—or foolishly!*

key point
MONEY CAN WORK FOR US.

Saving and investing are two good ways to use money wisely and put it to work for us. Saving money is wise—saving with interest is wiser. Encourage your younger child to save money in a piggy bank or jar. But help your older child set up a savings account that pays interest and he will see how his money earns even more!

TIPS FOR TODDLERS

Let your toddler help decorate a bank, then give him a penny each day to place in the bank. Tell him that when he gets to five or ten pennies, they can be traded for a shiny nickel or dime. This encourages saving and also helps counting skills! (Be sure to keep the bank out of reach so coins aren't "deposited" in the mouth!)

key point
IT'S SMART TO SAVE AND INVEST OUR MONEY.

Investing is similar to savings. Instead of simply putting your money in a bank, investing means placing your money in a larger company that uses the money to grow. When companies grow, they earn even more money and your investments grow as well. Higher rates of return often mean higher risks, so be sure you invest your money in a safe, reputable place.

BIG BIBLE POINT

Read Matthew 25:27 with your child, then ask:

• What does this verse teach us about using our money?
• Why is it wise to save with interest and not hide money?
• Why is it good for money to multiply?
• What can our money be used for?

Working, saving, investing—it can be confusing for kids! How can you show your child how putting something to work can multiply it? Make popcorn! Measure out one-half cup of popcorn kernels. Pop the popcorn, then measure how many cups you now have. Point out how the popcorn multiplied! Compare this to how money multiplies when you save and invest it with interest.

THE BIGGER THE RISK THE BIGGER THE RETURN— BUT WATCH OUT OR YOU COULD LOSE IT ALL!

Money is a tool that can build or destroy.

Just like a hammer, money is a tool. It can be used to build many great things, but one slip and that hammer can land on your thumb and create pain. Money is as much a driving force in our society today as it was so many years ago, and we will never be able to acquire the spiritual blessings God has for us until we learn to be "trustworthy in handling worldly wealth" (Luke 16:11).

key point
MONEY CAN BUILD.

When we realize that money is not an end in and of itself and is only a tool to help us build and enrich our lives, we become the good stewards God desires us to be. But what happens when money turns into a tool of destruction?

Some of us choose to go into debt in order to have our own way. Or perhaps we spend more than we have and can't meet our everyday financial responsibilities. When spending is out of control, the items that

once looked so desirable become great sorrows or weights. Before making any impulse buys, remind your child that being careful stewards with money demonstrates gratitude for what we already have.

key point
MONEY CAN DESTROY.

For a good review of how money used as a good tool multiplies, let your child help you bake bread! As the bread is set aside to rise (and "multiply"), remind your child that patience and a wise use of money helps it grow and become useful to us—just as bread doubles in size, then can be eaten to provide energy.

TARGET MOMENT

Get your child thinking about money in creative and positive ways. Discuss the following questions, keeping in mind that money is a tool to build or destroy.

• *If you had $100 right now, what would you do with it?*

• *Would you rather use money to build a school or buy a truckload of toys? Why?*

Challenge your child to identify household items that can used in both good and bad ways. For instance, the stove is a very useful tool when we want to cook dinner, yet if we're not careful it can cause pain with fires or burns. Helping your child to understand that money is a tool that can build or destroy sets up a lifetime of thoughtful respect for finances and carefully made choices when it comes to using money!

Think for a moment about your own finances and spending habits. Then ask yourself:

• *Do I often use credit? Why?*

• *Could I pay off my debts in 6 months?*

• *How are my debts keeping me from giving my family what they might need?*

• *Are my spending habits ones I want my kids to imitate?*

MONEY IS A USEFUL TOOL.

Money is not meant to be our master.

Money is not meant to be our master. Ask yourself: Is money my only goal in life? Remember that there are both good and bad consequences along with whatever choices you make.

We want to keep dollars and "sense" in perspective.

Matthew 6:24 states, "No one can serve two masters. Either he will hate the one and love the other, or he will be devoted to the one and despise the other. You cannot serve both God and Money." What a powerful verse that causes us to consider our attitudes and actions in regard to money. Money is a necessity and reality in our lives on earth, but money is also a tool to serve us—not the other way around!

key point
MONEY IS NOT TO BE SERVED!

Kids do need to know that money is not the most important thing in life. But it's so hard to teach them this when they see rock stars and sports figures making millions of dollars while teachers and ministers make just enough to get by. Kids and adults need to remember that money—and who we're to serve—must be kept in perspective!

DON'T FORGET

key point
MONEY ISN'T THE MOST IMPORTANT THING IN THE WORLD.

"A wise man should have money in his head, but not in his heart."

—Jonathan Swift

Notice how Matthew 6:24 capitalizes the M in the word "money"? It's as if God's Word is reminding us of the danger of placing money as a god in our lives. The Bible warns us to choose higher goals than money and to serve only God. Help your child make choices regarding money and how to keep dollars and sense in perspective!

"Do not store up for yourselves treasures on earth.... But store up for yourselves treasures in heaven.... For where your treasure is, there your heart will be also." (Matthew 6:19-21)

- *What treasures are you chasing after?*
- *What treasures are you building?*
- *Are your treasures temporary, or will they last forever?*
- *How can you work toward finding treasures of the heart?*

Encourage your child to think about things in life that make her smile or feel happy, such as her family, sunny days, fireworks, ice cream, helping others, and learning about Jesus. Cut out several paper hearts and "smiles" from construction paper. Then help your child write the things that give her joy on the paper shapes. Point out that money may be included in the list, but it is certainly not the only or most important thing in life. Tape the shapes around the room or hang them from a clothes hanger as reminders that money needs to be kept in a healthy perspective as God desires.

TIPS FOR 'TWEENS
On the left side of a paper, list things money can buy. On the other half, list things money can't buy, such as love, compassion, eternal life, and friendships. Compare lists, then point out how the treasures that endure forever are ones money can't buy!

Money can't buy good friends—they are treasures of the heart!

Money creates choices for us.

Money is a fact of life. We need it to survive and for the basic necessities in life. But even though money is a must, it still creates a myriad of choices. Will the things we need come before the things we want? Choices inspire decisions, and consequences come with every decision. The key is to make the right choices when it comes to spending, saving, and giving so that we realize good consequences from our decisions!

If kids are not encouraged or taught how to make wise choices, it can be detrimental to them as grown-ups. Adults who were never taught how to spend money usually find themselves deep in debt. Debt causes stress that may trickle down to family members, other relationships, or work. Being in debt causes a person to be a slave to the lender—or to debt itself!

PARENTS POINTER

Next time you write out a grocery list, use the categories of "needs" and "wants." Let your child help sort grocery items into the correct categories. Chat about the differences between a need and a want to emphasize that we have choices when shopping.

"THE RICH RULE OVER THE POOR, AND THE BORROWER IS SERVANT TO THE LENDER" (PROVERBS 22:7).

Kids often think that as grown-ups we can do whatever we want to do. They even may believe that if you go to a bank, the nice people there just *give* you money. Oh, for the faith of a child! Kids simply haven't experienced debt or late bill payments from mismanagement of money.

TIPS FOR TODDLERS

Cut out two colorful paper "coins" to hand your toddler next time you visit the grocery store. Explain that the paper coins are to allow your child two choices for special treats or wants they may have such as a favorite cookie or her very own apple!

key point
MONEY CREATES CHOICES.

key point
USING MONEY HAS CONSEQUENCES.

TRY THIS!

Get two sheets of paper and label one "Needs" and the other "Wants." Challenge your child to list or draw pictures of needs and wants in his life. Then discuss and prioritize his needs and wants by numbering them. Point out that needs should be met before wants are considered.

In a month when you have an extra $5, give your child the choice of how this money is to be spent. List out possibilities, from buying a new toy to buying $5 worth of canned goods for a local food bank. Discuss the pros and cons of each choice and who would benefit most, then let your child make the final decision. Discuss the decision that was made and how it felt to make that choice.

How We Get Money

We earn money through hard work, gifts, bonuses, or interest from investments we make. And though there are various ways to get money, one thing is certain: It's harder to come by than it is to spend!

Making money requires a plan.

The choices people make about money are very personal. Because people have different needs and wants, it is important to create a plan about how you'll earn money and what you'll do with it once it's in your possession.

Money doesn't "grow on trees."

Money doesn't grow on trees, but wouldn't it be nice if it did? Kids often think that money is easy to come by, that there's always enough, and that most people can afford to buy whatever they want. Including your child in family budgeting plans begins to provide a good idea of how we receive and use our money.

key point
MONEY IS HARD TO GET AND EASY TO LOSE.

DID YOU KNOW?

Money doesn't grow on trees—and even the paper for money isn't made of wood! Kids might be interested to know that paper bills today are made of 25 percent linen and 75 percent cotton fibers. Prior to World War I, the fibers were made of silk!

So where does money come from? Most people earn money by working at jobs. Some people may receive help from the government to pay their bills. And others who may have lost a job receive unemployment benefits.

If you bend down to pick up a penny, your children learn that even small amounts are to be treasured!

BIG BIBLE POINT

Read Ecclesiastes 5:11 aloud, then discuss the following questions:

- *What do you think this verse teaches us?*
- *Why is it good that people don't have everything they want?*
- *Is it good to earn or work for money? Explain.*
- *How can we be thankful for what we have instead of always wanting more?*

In this age of instant credit, debit cards, and "plastic money," it's often confusing for kids who think money is like an unending river! Point out that banks don't simply *give away* money and that checks, no matter how easy to write, are not limitless—they're good only for the amount of money you have in the bank.

Create a family money tree. Tape real tree branches to the front of the refrigerator. Cut out paper leaves. As a family, write on the leaves needs and wants for the month, including everything from rent to eating out. Tape the leaves to the branches, then remove a leaf each time a listed need or want is met. Discuss the importance of meeting needs before wants.

Careful planning makes good "cents."

Do you spend money on the things you want before you spend it on what you need? Teaching your child how to be a responsible spender is a necessity and a skill to last his whole life long. Showing your child how to keep track of how much money she has and whether or not she can afford her wants teaches the secrets to success with money!

A budget can help kids—and adults—manage money more effectively. The first step is to help your child understand what a budget is and how one works. Explain that a budget is a written plan that shows how much money is coming in and how much money is being spent and where it is being spent. Point out that budgets provide useful information to help save for the future and to cut wasteful spending. It might be a real eye-opener to share with your child your own budget to give him an idea of what it costs each month for your house or the family food bill, or how much extra items like a new pair of shoes or school supplies cost. Kids are usually in awe of how much is spent on everyday items!

TARGET MOMENT

Some kids may find it helpful to use a series of labeled envelopes to apportion their money. For example, one envelope might be labeled Fun Money and hold the money for movies, CDs, or treats. Another envelope might be Savings and hold the money set aside to save until your trip to the bank, and so on.

key point

BUDGETS HELP MANAGE MONEY.

BUDGETS HELP
S-T-R-E-T-C-H
DOLLARS—PASS ON GOOD
BUDGETING HABITS!

SIMPLE BUDGETS HELP MANAGE MONEY!

Matthew's Budget for January

Money Coming In

Allowance	$10.00
Scooping Snow	$5.00
Birthday Money	$25.00
Total	**$40.00**

Money Going Out

Spending - Model Car	$8.50
Sharing - Church	$4.00
Savings	$27.50
Total	**$40.00**

Help your child understand that there are two main parts to a budget: money coming in and money going out. The first part records income or money that is earned. The second part of a budget shows how money is used. It may include spending, saving, or donating. Budgeting becomes easier once your child understands that what he has to spend is *all* he has to spend!

If your child receives an allowance and has money coming in on a regular basis, help her create a simple budget. Remind her to include money that will be saved and not spent at all. Teach your child that to a balance a budget she must subtract money going out from money coming in. If she hits zero, the budget is balanced. Planning definitely makes good "cents"!

BUDGETS ARE LIKE SPENDING AND SAVING BLUEPRINTS!

- **Do you use a solid spending plan each month?**
- **Do you often "break" your budget with extra spending?**
- Do you purchase needs before wants?
- Are you regularly saving money?
- Are your budgeting habits ones you'd like your kids to imitate?

We make money through our work.

Did you earn an allowance as a child? Did you know what your parents did for a living and how much money they made? It's important for kids to realize that most work is rewarded with money but that, more importantly, all work is honorable.

Allowances teach about handling money.

Now that you have your own kids, you're faced with many allowance issues, such as how much to pay and whether your child will be allowed to buy whatever she wants. There are so many things to consider when making decisions about allowances!

key point
ALLOWANCES TEACH MONEY MANAGEMENT.

Allowances are a way for children to learn how to handle money. Children are usually ready for an allowance around six years of age. The allowance amount will vary, but some suggest using the "dollar-for-every-year-old" rule to determine allowance amounts. This is fine, but you'll probably want to increase the amount as your child gets older and has more needs.

key point
CHORES AREN'T ALWAYS REWARDED WITH MONEY!

TARGET MOMENT

In a recent poll by an organization dealing with kids' allowances, 19 percent of the parents asked considered 5-year-olds too young to receive a regular allowance.

ALLOWANCE DO'S & DONT'S

- **Do** *have your child save a portion of his allowance.*
- **Do** *give the same sum on the same day each week.*
- **Do** *discuss budgeting allowance money.*
- **Do** *let kids learn from their mistakes.*
- **Do** *let kids earn extra money doing special jobs.*
- **Do** *increase the allowance as kids get older.*
- **Don't** *give allowances as rewards.*
- **Don't** *control your child's buying.*
- **Don't** *use allowances as a punishment.*
- **Don't** *rule out helping with special spending needs.*

B y getting allowances, kids learn to plan spending. They realize the necessity of making good choices. They practice mathematics and logic with budgeting, saving, and what will be spent. Initially your child will make mistakes managing his allowance, but over time he will learn to be selective in his purchases and prudent in his spending!

W hatever your goals for allowances, help your child realize there are a certain number of household duties he is responsible for on a regular basis. These chores remind your child he is an active, productive member of your family "team" and that money doesn't always reward every bit of work we do!

AVERAGE ALLOWANCES

AGE	AMOUNT
3	$3.20
4	$2.85
5	$3.15
6	$3.85
7	$4.10
8	$4.32
9	$5.52
10	$7.18
11	$7.92
12	$9.38
13	$9.52

Global/Decima Parent Poll, 1997

WE MAKE MONEY THROUGH OUR WORK.

All work is honorable.

Do you ever feel as though some jobs just go unnoticed by your spouse, your employer, or even your kids? Our kids are no different when it comes to the jobs and chores they do. A simple "good job" or "I like the way you did this" can go miles in giving kids a feeling of pride and accomplishment. By taking the time to encourage your child in his "work," you begin to build the foundations of a healthy work ethic to last a lifetime!

Our attitudes surrounding our work, profession, bosses and co-workers, and work satisfaction—or lack thereof—are all noticed by our kids. All too often we communicate a spoken or unspoken message saying, "My job isn't worth anything." Whether you're doing a load of laundry or designing bridges, your work is worthy and honorable. And whether kids are delivering newspapers or taking out the trash, their work is honorable, too!

key point
HONEST WORK IS HONORABLE.

TIPS FOR TODDLERS

Make your toddler's job of picking up the play area more fun by counting the items he puts away. Hand toddlers toy brooms and fluffy feather dusters to help with cleaning chores!

Kids learn valuable lessons from working or helping out with daily chores. They learn how to manage time and to be organized. They learn responsibility while making a commitment and following through. Working may inspire your child to think about the future. Regardless of the type of work, job, or chore your child completes, he will begin to understand that all work is honorable and something to be proud of!

key point
WORKING TEACHES US MANY THINGS.

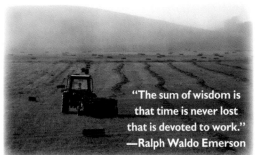

"The sum of wisdom is that time is never lost that is devoted to work."
—Ralph Waldo Emerson

Make a chart showing what large and small household jobs your child can do. Assign a value to each job, but don't limit the value to monetary rewards only. For example, one job may earn money, while another earns a special home-cooked meal. Discuss why certain jobs were or weren't chosen. Was it because one job seemed better than another? Remind your child that all honest work, regardless of the job or pay, is honorable if it's done well!

Read aloud Proverbs 14:23 and 21:25 with your child. Then discuss the following questions.

- *What are the rewards of work?*
- *Are the rewards always monetary? Explain.*
- *What happens to those who are lazy?*
- *Why is all work pleasing to God?*
- *How can the work of your hands delight your heart?*

What messages do you give your child about work?

We make money by selling goods and services.

Even when kids receive an allowance, they always want more. One way to do this is to supplement allowances by working outside the home selling newspapers, washing cars, or doing yardwork.

Talents can translate into cash.

We can receive money through gifts, by way of working, through interest from bank accounts, and from allowances. People also get money through goods they sell and services they provide. One of the best ways to discover the worth of goods and services is through our interests and talents!

key point
GOD GIVES US SPECIAL TALENTS.

key point
TALENTS CAN BECOME GOODS AND SERVICES.

It seems that as we grow older we lose sight of the talents God has given us. Helping your child discover what he is good at is an invaluable gift that can serve him well financially later in life. Whatever our hobbies, interests, or talents, people find unique ways to put their talents to work earning cash—and that's an interest all kids (and adults) share!

TIPS FOR 'TWEENS
If your child is ready to be an entrepreneur, have him create a flyer with a catchy phrase offering his services for yard cleaning, dog walking, car washing, or any number of services. Hand them to friends and family. Who knows? Your child may start a booming business!

Using talents can turn goods and services into cash—in fun ways! If your child likes cooking, he might sell brownies at a bake sale. Crafty kids can make greeting cards. Each of us has talents that God has given, and we can often use these talents to earn a living—or at least a bit of extra cash!

KIDS LOVE THINKING UP FUN WAYS TO EARN A FEW DOLLARS.

If your child is interested in making more money than he does from his allowance, discuss what talents he has and how he might turn those talents into cash around your home or even around town. Create a "business plan" together and encourage your child to follow through on it. There are many examples of kids starting with a simple talent and turning it into a thriving business later in life. Encourage your child to be creative!

TARGET MOMENT

"Each one should use whatever gifts he has received to serve others, faithfully administering God's grace in its various forms" (1 Peter 4:10). **Use your talents wisely!**

TRY THIS!

Help your child understand that God-given talents don't just need to be used to acquire money—they can be used instead of money to help others! Look for ways to donate your talents and time. For instance, cooking talents might be used to bake cookies for a homeless shelter, or artistic talents might be used to make cards for kids in a hospital.

Turn talents into pocket money.

Time can translate into cash.

With a little time and patience, time can translate into money in several ways. Interest from assets, stocks, and bonds can grow and become more valuable over time. Money held in savings accounts, certificates of deposit, and money-market funds can also accumulate more over months and years. But the quickest and easiest way time increases money is by giving our personal time to offer and provide worthwhile services.

There are a number of ways kids can use their time to earn or make money. Yardwork, including raking leaves, weeding gardens, and mowing lawns, is a great way for kids to offer their time in exchange for money. Girls enjoy babysitting if they're old enough and may enjoy bathing dogs or taking them for walks. In exchange for time spent doing a chore or job well, they receive monetary compensation; they're trading their time for money.

TARGET MOMENT

What do you think Benjamin Franklin meant when he said, "Remember that time is money"?

key point
PROVIDING SERVICES HELPS OTHERS.

Look in the jobs section of the newspaper to find what types of jobs are needed and what they pay. Figure out what someone would make if she received $10 an hour and worked all day.

What can your child learn from offering his time by providing services to others? Plenty! Offering time for odd jobs helps others who may not be able to do the jobs themselves. Elderly neighbors appreciate someone to shovel and sweep the walk for them and may even toss in a few cookies as "bonus" pay! Kids offering services learn that jobs need to be done well and not to let people down.

key point
TIME CAN BE TRADED FOR CASH.

Encourage your child to experiment with trading his time for cash. Make posters to hang around the neighborhood, tell friends, or distribute flyers to help your child advertise the new "business." Encourage him to decide what he'll charge for his time. Help him understand that it's important to be on time, to be thorough, to be a cheerful worker, and to be businesslike. Children need guidance and support with their first enterprises but will soon understand how time and services translate into cash once they receive that first payment for services rendered!

TIPS FOR 'TWEENS
Contract with your older child to "employ" her for certain tasks. Give an expected due date for completing the job and have your child sign the agreement. When the jobs are done and the payments made, discuss how hourly wages work.

+ TALENTS = $$$

(TIME PLUS TALENTS EQUALS MONEY!)

We receive money through gifts.

Not only people receive money through gifts, but so do churches, nonprofit organizations, and some businesses. Monetary gifts are wonderful to receive and can often help people and organizations accomplish their goals and dreams.

Monetary gifts are like gifts of grace.

God's grace abounds to us from His love and through nothing we've done to deserve it. When we offer monetary gifts to a church, an organization, someone needy, or even our own kids on special occasions, we're giving gifts of grace—monetary gifts from our own love to someone regardless of if he deserves the gift.

Churches must pay their employees, their bills, for the building itself, and for the Bibles and supplies they use. Nonprofit organizations such as homeless shelters, food banks, or orphanages depend on gifts of grace to meet their expenditures. Just imagine these kinds of service organizations without monetary gifts of grace people like you offer!

key point
MONETARY GIFTS ARE LIKE GRACE.

COFFEE BREAK

- How do you feel about donating to others?
- What "gifts of grace" can you give this week?
- How can you model acts of giving to your child?

BIG BIBLE POINT

Help your child understand that God loves a cheerful (and generous) giver. Read aloud 2 Corinthians 9:6, 7, then discuss the following:

- What does God say about giving?
- Do we need to worry that we're giving too much? Explain.
- What does God promise if we're generous? if we're stingy?
- How does being a generous giver show love for God?

Over a snack and a cup of juice, engage your child in a lively discussion of which she would rather do if she had $1,000 and why: spend the money, save it, or donate it to someone in need. Be sure to share your own ideas for what you'd do!

Birthday dollars, coins tucked under pillows for lost teeth, or even donations to homeless people bring as much joy to the giver as they do to the receiver! Remind your child that how much is given is not as important as the attitude in which gifts of grace are offered! Paul reminds us in 2 Corinthians 9:7 that "God loves a cheerful giver."

As a family, make it a goal to give of your money, time, or other donations to help someone less fortunate than you. Save money to buy food baskets for rescue missions. Donate your gifts of money or time to a local soup kitchen. Help your child experience the warmth that comes from selfless gifts of grace!

key point
GIVE WITH AN ATTITUDE OF LOVE!

Money requires a thankful attitude.

We know that God is pleased when we give or donate to others with an attitude of joy and love. But having an attitude of gratitude is just as important when receiving money or any other gifts! There are countless ways to express our gratitude and thanksgiving for all we've received, and giving back to God and others is one way. It's important for children to understand that giving is not just a way to thank God for the blessings in life but is a way to trust God's love and care.

Kids as well as many adults sometimes find themselves overcome by three "Money Monsters": stinginess, greed, and ingratitude. We forget that it's wanting what we have that counts—not having what we want all the time! The Money Monsters stop kids from feeling joy and expressing their thankfulness as they should.

key point
BE THANKFUL FOR WHAT YOU HAVE.

How can we express our gratitude for what God has given? Read aloud with your child the parable of the Widow's Offering from Mark 12:41-44. Then discuss the following questions:

- *Why did the widow give more than the rich people?*

- *How did giving to God express her thanks?*

- *What can we learn about giving from this story? about expressing our thanks?*

"God gave you a gift of 86,400 seconds today. Have you used one to say "thank you"?
—William A. Ward

So what does having a spirit of thankfulness do for your child? It allows him to feel truly thankful for what he has and creates the desire to share his good fortune. Gratitude creates a warm feeling of gratefulness inside his heart and allows him to express his love to God. Giving produces thankfulness, which in turn produces more giving—what a wonderful cycle of gratitude your child can have!

Remind your child that thankfulness is expressed through our actions and not just in saying the words. Hebrews 13:5 says, "Keep your lives free from the love of money and be content with what you have." Help your child express his gratitude by serving, giving, sharing, and being content with what he has!

PRAYER EXPRESSES OUR THANKS TO GOD.

An attitude of gratitude encourages your child to think of others who may not have as much—as well as how he can help.

Create a collage of thanks by gluing pictures of things you're thankful for on the top half of a sheet of poster board. On the bottom half, write a simple poem that expresses contentment with what you have.

We make money through interest.

Have you ever heard Ben Franklin's wise saying that "a penny saved is a penny earned"? That's wise advice, but it's even wiser when the penny saved is gaining interest, which is like getting free money—and everyone loves free stuff!

Interest is like free money.

Banks are generally good, safe places to keep your money. When a deposit is made to a savings account, the bank uses it to make more money. Banks combine your money with other people's money to create loans for others. In return for using your money, banks pay you interest—kind of like a rental fee for using your money!

key point
EARNING INTEREST IS WISE!

key point
SAVE MONEY WHERE IT EARNS INTEREST.

PIGGY BANKS ARE CUTE, BUT THEY DON'T ALLOW MONEY TO GROW.

In its most simple form, a bank uses your saved money by lending it to someone who needs a loan for a house, car, or other large purchase. The borrower then pays the bank for letting him use the money. When you have a savings account, interest is good and is like "free money" the bank pays you. But if you are the borrower, *you* are paying interest to the bank—and that's not free money!

Eating healthy and exercising keeps us fit and trim, which are good physical goals to have. And making a healthy habit of saving money with interest allows us to reach our financial goals. When our money receives interest, it earns more than sitting in a cute piggy bank or a sock.

Exercise good financial fitness—save with interest!

Remind your child that putting money in the bank is definitely a good way to save money. But another good way is to curb spending!

Is your child ready to open a savings account? If she has been receiving an allowance on a regular basis or has a piggy bank that needs emptying, take her to the bank to open a savings account or certificate of deposit that pays interest. Have your child count the money she is saving and write the amount along with the date in a special notebook.

Many banks or savings and loans will provide a nifty bank book with your child's name on it so you can record additional deposits and interest earnings. Explain that money left in the bank will grow into more money. This will help your child see how interest earnings work—and motivate her to continue saving!

TRY THIS!

Grab some crayons, marshmallows, and a coloring book. Divide the crayons and hand each person five marshmallows. When you want to borrow a crayon, you must "pay" one marshmallow to use it. Compare how many marshmallows you have after coloring. Did you spend or "earn" more marshmallows and why?

Interest is money at work for us.

There are three types of savings accounts that would be great starting places for your child to put his money to work earning interest. A simple savings account is the most common and is found at most banks and savings and loans. Statements are sent to you and your child that show how much money is in the account.

A "nest" savings account is also called a "passbook" account. The bank teller records each transaction in a little book, including deposits, withdrawals, and interest. Kids love having their own passbooks to look at, and they may help encourage your child to keep saving! Most kids feel a real sense of pride over their savings accounts when they can actually see the numbers in the passbook. It's a great concrete reminder of how their money is growing and working for them!

TIPS FOR 'TWEENS

Have some math fun with your older child! Let's say you put $10 in a bank with a 5 percent annual interest rate. This means the bank will pay 5¢ per dollar every year. At the end of the first year, 50¢ will have been earned, for a total of $10.50 in your account. How much interest will be earned if you put $100 in the bank? $1,000?

key point
MAKE MONEY WORK FOR YOU.

Putting Your Money to Work for You!

Weekly Savings	After 1 Year	After 2 Years	After 3 Years
$5	$266.32	$545.96	$839.58
$10	$532.64	$1,091.92	$1,679.16
$15	$798.97	$1,637.88	$2,518.74
$20	$1,065.29	$2,183.34	$3,358.32
$25	$1,331.61	$2,729.80	$4,197.90

This chart shows how saving just $5, $10, $15, $20, or $25 a week can grow at a rate of 5 percent interest.

The last type of savings accounts is called a certificate of deposit or CD. This is a great account for kids who receive larger money gifts for birthdays or holidays and who are not planning to use the money for several

months or years. The money cannot be withdrawn until the end of the specified time period, but money earns higher interest than other accounts earn!

Encourage your child to put his money to work by earning interest. Tell him that you will match the bank's interest rate on what he has earned each month. For example, if the bank paid your child $1 for the month of March, you would also give her $1 to add to her account. Each time you view the new and growing balance, remind your child that it's great when money works for us!

How We Use Money

Money provides many of the necessary things in life if we choose to use it in healthy ways! Creating positive models for saving, spending, and donating money will encourage your child to make good decisions when it comes to using money.

Money provides things we need.

Money is an important tool when meeting our needs. Shelter, clothing, food, and transportation are all items we must pay for, and without money we wouldn't be able to provide these or other key necessities in life.

We must prioritize our needs.

DON'T FORGET

Consider your spiritual needs when assessing your family's needs and how to use money to meet them. Tithing at church or donating to a special church mission or project uses your money in a wonderful and much-needed way!

Financial planning for today, tomorrow, and our futures requires prioritizing of our needs. When we prioritize our needs, we're making choices that affect us today and tomorrow. Kids need to understand the basic choices of either spending within their budgets, choosing to go into debt, or doing without. We make these important choices each time we use money.

Sadly, too many people spend too little time focusing on the choices and consequences surrounding money. It's important to remind your child that there are three basic ways to use money: spend it, save it, or donate it. Prioritizing how you plan to use your money can prevent it from being "nickel and dimed" away!

key point
PRIORITIZE NEEDS BEFORE WANTS.

key point
LIVING CREATES CERTAIN NEEDS.

Use family expenses as a great example of prioritizing needs. Write down family needs, then prioritize the top ten on your list. As you discuss your priorities, ask questions such as "What makes food more of a priority than having new clothes to wear?" or "Why do you think we should meet our needs before using money to buy toys, trips, or movies?" Communicating about the needs of your family can open up your child's eyes about important priorities and using money wisely.

TIPS FOR 'TWEENS
Invite your older child to go on a virtual shopping trip using the Internet or a store catalog. Tell him he has $200 to spend, save, or donate. Make a budget and list the expenditures. Remind your child that using money on what's most important is a wise use of finances!

We must budget for our needs.

If you are serious about gaining control of your own finances and preparing for the future, budgeting is a must! A budget only works if it's well planned out and adhered to. A budget is simply an effective tool to help organize your life and manage your money more efficiently. If you desire to establish healthy money habits with your child, it's important to evaluate and use a solid budget of your own!

Just as prioritizing our needs puts our lives into perspective, budgeting puts our spending into perspective. Budgets help you buy or meet your highest priorities without wasting money or frittering it away on items that are frivolous wants instead of needs. The amount of money you put in your monthly budget should be equal to the amount of income you have from your paycheck. Setting up a budget isn't too difficult—but limiting your spending may be! If you have more money going out than planned or than you brought in, you could be in serious trouble meeting your needs!

TIPS FOR 'TWEENS
Try offering a "matching funds award" if your child reaches a predetermined savings goal within a certain amount of time. For example, if your 'tween saves $30 in six months, match that amount!

Kids love handling money, but help them handle it wisely.

Sometimes unforeseen events happen that we must be ready for. Yes, you need this item and you need that item—but what happens when your spouse loses her job and you can't afford this and that? If you have money saved, this shouldn't be a problem while he searches for a new job. If there's money saved, this should lessen any problems. Kids need to remember the importance of saving for "rainy days" as they budget for their needs today and for emergencies tomorrow.

BIG BIBLE POINT

Sticking to a budget helps us use money to buy the things we need. Read aloud Isaiah 55:2 to your child, then discuss the following:

- *What does this verse mean?*
- *Is it wise to use money for what's needed? Explain.*
- *Can money be used only for what's needed? Explain.*
- *If you're hungry, why is it better to spend for food than for a new toy?*
- *How can we help meet the needs of others by our own wise spending?*

key point

BUDGETS HELP CONTROL SPENDING.

key point

WE MUST RECOGNIZE OUR NEEDS.

Whether it's a weekly or monthly budget, encourage your child to stick to it. Budgeting takes practice! You wouldn't send your child to perform in a piano recital if she had never touched a keyboard before, and using money wisely is no different. With a bit of patience and guidance, your child will be able to create and stick to a budget that prepares her to use money wisely!

Wise parents "practice what they preach." If you expect your kids to stick to their budgets, don't forget to stick to your own family budget as well!

Money provides things we want.

Not only does money provide for the things we need, but it also provides for things we desire or dream of. Spending requires a sense of responsibility and planning, but it's okay to budget for our desires as well—as long as we're spending within our means.

Spending requires responsibility.

Needs versus wants. It's a never-ending decision of what to spend our resources on. Some choices are easy. We need to provide a place to live, food to eat, and clothing for our families. But other choices can be more difficult to make. Is it really okay to want a new car when the older one runs fine? Our desires, dreams, and wants are often causes for guilt. Spending money on desires and wants is fine, but learning to be responsible spenders is the key!

TARGET MOMENT

Did you know that some marketing experts have designated kids as the newest market with dollars to spend? In addition, they claim kids influence about $600 billion in family-spending dollars!

Giving children an allowance teaches them about careful spending. Let your third grader know that she is now responsible for buying pencils or paper from her weekly allowance. If she spends too much money on candy, she will need to use old pencils or borrow one. Your child must be allowed to make mistakes in spending—mistakes she can learn from.

CANDY IS DANDY, BUT ALL CHOICES COME WITH A COST.

Parents often wonder what they should do when their child's allowance runs out too soon. Do you cave in and give him more cash? Generally you should allow your child to take responsibility for his spending, and if he spends too much or too quickly, he needs to feel the reality of being broke. Your child will learn about self-control and self-restraint by experiencing limitations. Your child will have no reason to plan ahead or discipline his spending if he is given extra money once his is gone.

key point
SPEND SENSIBLY!

Because children today are consumers at such an early age, they need to experience the importance of good financial choices. If your daughter wants to go to a movie with her friends and buy soda and popcorn but only has enough for the movie, she has to make a choice. She can either go next week after she has saved more money or can enjoy the movie and eat at home later.

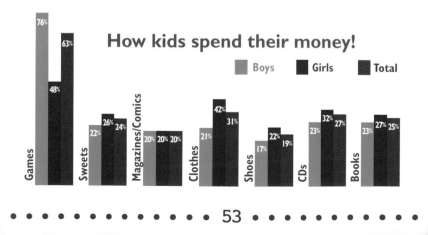

How kids spend their money!

Boys Girls Total

- Games: 76%, 63%, 48%
- Sweets: 22%, 26%, 24%
- Magazines/Comics: 20%, 20%, 20%
- Clothes: 21%, 42%, 31%
- Shoes: 17%, 22%, 19%
- CDs: 23%, 32%, 27%
- Books: 23%, 27%, 25%

Too much spending is dangerous.

Have you ever bought something and then thought to yourself, "Oh no! What have I done?" We all enjoy driving nice cars, living in beautiful homes, and owning items that let us live comfortable lives. But when spending goes outside our means, it becomes dangerous and destructive. People who don't use and stick to budgets or who don't regularly prioritize their needs usually find themselves in debt.

Some debt is necessary. For example, most people cannot afford to pay cash for a house, a car, or a college education. But when we're spoiled, unable to delay gratification, or try to keep up with the Joneses, spending becomes dangerous. Cash is depleted or credit cards may be charged until, before you know it, you're up to your eyeballs in debt—and repossession may mean the loss of that new car we just "couldn't resist"!

key point
WISE SPENDING REQUIRES PATIENCE!

key point
DEBT CAN BE DESTRUCTIVE.

Are your own spending habits under control? Do you use credit too often instead of exercising patience? Your child watches not only what you buy but how you pay for it. Choose and use credit carefully. The more you model "patience in purchasing," the more your child will, too!

"Never spend your money before you have it!"
—Thomas Jefferson

Most kids are into instant gratification and find it tough to be patient while saving money. But good things come to those who wait! Remind your child that we may not be able to delay spending for our needs, but we do have control over what we spend for our wants!

TRY THIS!

To reinforce the fact that spending requires responsible choices, ask your child to tell you what possible consequences there would be if …

• *you spent your house payment or rent.*

• *you spent your food money.*

• *you didn't have money for the bus.*

• *you couldn't pay back a loan to the bank.*

• *you spent your movie ticket money.*

Make a menu similar to the one on this page, then give your child $50 in play money to "spend" during the coming week. Will your child blow all his money on a favorite movie and popcorn? At the end of the week, chat about the spending decisions and why they were made. Remind your child that spending comes with responsibilities and consequences—and the choices are up to him!

Your Choice Money Menu!

Watch favorite movie	$2.00
Favorite cooked meal	$3.00
Dinner out	$10.00
Ride to school	$7.00
Stay up extra 30 minutes	$7.00
Extra bedtime story read	$2.00
Don't have to make bed	$5.00

Plastic money isn't always good to use.

Plastic money is a misnomer, as it is really debt instead of cash. Our kids are used to seeing plastic used for credit and cards for cash. Even toddlers play with plastic cards, swiping them across books as they pretend to pay for play groceries. Plastic money creates confusion in kids and a false sense of reality about what's affordable and what isn't.

key point
BUYING WITH CASH IS SMART!

Read aloud Exodus 22:25, then discuss the following questions with your child:

- *What would happen if banks and businesses didn't charge us interest for borrowing money?*

- *Would people pay back their debt in a timely manner? Explain.*

- *How can we spend wisely and be good stewards with our money?*

Explain that a debit card is used to pull existing money directly out of a savings or checking account but that a credit card is used as a loan for money you may not have in the bank. It must be paid back with interest and will add even more money to what you owe. Help your child understand that using credit cards is like taking out a loan that must be paid back quickly—or interest rates will add even more money to what you owe.

key point
CREDIT CREATES QUICK DEBT.

When you scramble the letters in the word "owe," you find the word "woe," which means trouble and sorrow!

$1,000 CASH = $1,575 CREDIT

{ IF YOU CHARGE $1,000 AT 5 PER-
CENT INTEREST AND MAKE A $20
PAYMENT EACH MONTH, IT WILL
TAKE YOU OVER 6 YEARS TO PAY
IT BACK—AND YOU'LL PAY BACK
ALMOST $600 MORE! }

It's amazing to realize that kids as young as sixteen are being sent applications for credit cards—and even more amazing when the typical credit-card debt of the average eighteen- to twenty-year-old is nearing $6,000! Clearly we need to help our kids realize that instant cash from plastic money is dangerous and can ruin their chances at financial freedom early in life.

When you use your debit card, explain that the card allows you to use cash right from your account—that it's subtracted from your account immediately just as cash is instantly gone when it's spent. When you're tempted to charge a "want," think again and explain to your child that it's probably better to make the purchase when you have the cash instead of running up debt. A good rule of thumb is: If you have to charge it, you probably don't need it!

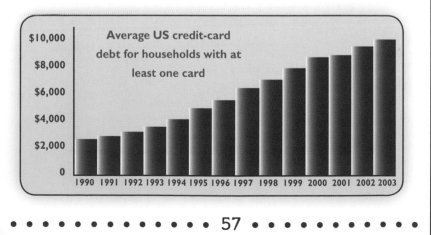

Average US credit-card debt for households with at least one card

Money provides care for others.

So many people are in need around the world, and monetary donations from those who are generous help care for these people. Whether it's money for food and medicine or for rebuilding after a natural disaster, giving from the goodness of our hearts helps others in so many ways—physically, emotionally, financially, and spiritually.

Donations help the needy in many ways.

The power of people who have hearts—and money—to share can be amazing! Immediately following the devastating Asian tsunami of 2004, countless countries and individuals from all over the world donated millions of dollars, without which many survivors would not have lived and wouldn't have been able to begin rebuilding what was lost.

key point
PEOPLE HAVE POWER TO HELP OTHERS.

Encourage your child to nurture a sense of compassion when it comes to helping people in your community. Donating a portion of his allowance to a local food bank or to a needy family at church allows your child to put compassion into action—just as Jesus desired of us when He said, "Feed my sheep" (John 21:17).

- How many donations do you make each year?
- What are ways your donations help others? help you?
- Could you sacrifice the price of one cup of coffee a day to help others in need?

TARGET MOMENT

Through the Heifer Project, your child or entire family can purchase an animal—or an ark full of animals—for a needy third-world village! Go to www.heifer.org to check out the very reasonable prices or write to: Heifer Project International, P.O. Box 8058, Little Rock, AR/USA 72203. This is a donation your child will never forget—and neither will needy villagers!

Explain that many service organizations distribute food and clothing and provide shelter to the homeless or needy—and that we can help by donating a portion of our money to them. Organizations such as the Salvation Army and Habitat for Humanity actively help people facing hard times get back on their feet again. Remind kids that monetary donations help the needy but also create a sense of community—and may change someone's life forever!

key point
DONATING SHOWS COMPASSION.

Decorate a special box or jar or embellish a piggy bank using plastic jewels and paints. Then encourage your whole family to save money each week. After a few months, buy nonperishable food items for a food bank or soup kitchen. Or consider purchasing a pig, rabbit, or chicken for a needy village through Heifer International (see the Target Moment). What a memory maker!

> **"Let us not be satisfied with just giving money. . . . They need your hearts to love them."**
> **—Mother Teresa**

Be generous—not greedy!

How many times have you asked your kids to share their toys or take turns on the swing with their siblings or friends? In essence, you're asking your child to be generous with his turns—not greedy. It's often quite a challenge to convince toddlers and preschoolers to share. If you think greed is only a childhood dilemma, think again. Humans are inherently self-centered and are born seeking nothing more than meeting their own physical needs. The challenge is how to steer our kids toward generosity and away from greed!

key point
GOD OWNS ALL WE HAVE.

God's Word teaches us to be on guard against all kinds of greed, envy, and jealousy. In fact, Jesus Himself tells us that "man's life does not consist in the abundance of his possessions" (Luke 12:15). Greed is the absence of sharing and, ultimately, the absence of caring. Help your child realize that generosity and sharing are keys to friendships, to a peaceful heart, and to serving and obeying God!

key point
GREED IS SELF-DESTRUCTIVE.

TIPS FOR TODDLERS
The concept of sharing often feels so permanent to a young child! Try saying "let's take turns" instead of "let's share." It helps toddlers and preschoolers realize that their toys will return to them after a friend or sibling has a turn.

"A generous man will prosper; he who refreshes others will himself be refreshed" **(Proverbs 11:25).**

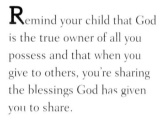

If greed is the absence of sharing, then generosity is the abundance of caring! Sometimes kids are afraid to share, fearing loss of what they have. Assure your child that God desires us to be generous and promises we will be made "rich in every way" (2 Corinthians 9:11).

BIG BIBLE POINT

The book of Proverbs offers much instruction about greed and generosity. Read aloud these verses with your kids, then discuss what each teaches us about being generous or greedy:

- *"A heart at peace gives life to the body, but envy rots the bones"* *(Proverbs 14:30).*

- *"A generous man will prosper"* *(Proverbs 11:25).*

- *"A generous man will himself be blessed, for he shares his food with the poor" (Proverbs 22:9).*

- *"A greedy man brings trouble to his family" (Proverbs 15:27).*

Remind your child that God is the true owner of all you possess and that when you give to others, you're sharing the blessings God has given you to share.

Thumb through catalogs and cut out gifts your child would like to "give" to each family member. Glue the pictures for each person to a sheet of construction paper and add a loving "gift card" to each one before presenting them to family members. Remind your child that God loves a cheerful (and generous) giver!

MONEY PROVIDES CARE FOR OTHERS.

Money provides ways to serve God.

Regardless of how much or how little we have, generosity, the desire to donate to those in need, and how we use our money to serve God all reflect who we are—and the conditions of our hearts.

God loves a cheerful giver.

Ask your child what his response would be if someone gave him the most wonderful gift imaginable. He would probably respond with a heartfelt "thank you!" And our response to God's perfect provision should be no less.

Invite your child to make a thank-you card for God. Decorate the front of the card using crayons, markers, or craft scraps. Then encourage your child to write a few lines thanking God for His gifts and telling one way your child can give to God in the coming week.

key point
BE A CHEERFUL GIVER!

key point
GIVING SERVES GOD.

"SERVE ONE ANOTHER IN LOVE" (GALATIANS 5:13).

Our loving expressions of thanks to God for all He has given should include living lives that serve God and giving back to Him. Giving through offerings and tithes at church are ways we can use money to thank and serve God. And God wants us to give freely—not with a spirit of stinginess or begrudging obligation.

BIG BIBLE POINT

"Each man should give what he has decided in his heart to give, not reluctantly or under compulsion, for God loves a cheerful giver" (2 Corinthians 9:7). Read this verse aloud, then discuss the following questions:

• What does being a cheerful giver mean to you?

• Are you a cheerful giver? Explain.

• How can you give cheerfully to God this week? to others?

Reassure your child that God doesn't measure our thanks by the amount of money we give in an offering plate but rather by the heart and spirit in which it's given. And the best part? Proverbs 11:25 tells us that God promises to bless, refresh, and prosper those who give generously and joyously.

Make a list with your child of all the ways God has blessed your family. Include the physical gifts God has given you such as a safe place to live and good food to enjoy, as well as talents and other spiritual gifts you're blessed with. Teaching your child to recognize what he's been given and to respond through cheerful giving helps nurture an attitude of gratitude and a spirit of thanksgiving.

"Remember that the happiest people are not those getting more, but those giving more."
—H. Jackson Brown Jr.

Tithing honors God.

Long ago in Old Testament times, tithes were centered around animal and agricultural products and was paid in like kind, not in money. Because the word *tithe* in Hebrew means "one-tenth," the tithe became linked to the figure of 10 percent. Tithing and offering to God became ways to honor, thank, and worship Him.

Tithes and offerings are two of the most basic activities for Christians, included among prayer, worship, and witnessing the Good News about Jesus. But how much does the Bible tell us we should tithe or give? According to 2 Corinthians 9:7, "Each man should give what he has decided in his heart to give, not reluctantly or under compulsion, for God loves a cheerful giver." And in the preceding verse we're told that "whoever sows sparingly will also reap sparingly, and whoever sows generously will also reap generously."

key point

TITHING HONORS AND THANKS GOD.

"Through Jesus, therefore, let us continually offer to God a sacrifice of praise"
(Hebrews 13:15).

Your tithes help Christ's church grow, provide for church leaders, and support missionaries.

Invite your child to help separate out 10 percent of the produce you grow in a garden and donate it to a food bank, or pull out 10 percent (or more) of the groceries you just purchased to give to a homeless shelter! Remind your child that tithing doesn't always need to be in dollars, that giving to honor God comes in many forms!

SHARE THE BOUNTY AND HONOR GOD!

Help your child understand more about giving to God by encouraging him to give an allowance "tithe" to the offering plate each Sunday. If your child receives an allowance of $3 each week, he could tithe 30¢ of his allowance. Remind your child that when we offer to God of what He has given us, we're helping serve both the church and God. Remind your child that wanting to give back to God is a natural extension of our love for Him—and that our tithes and offerings invite God's blessings to flow to others and to us!

key point
AS YOU GIVE TO GOD, HE GIVES TO YOU!

TIPS FOR 'TWEENS
Challenge your older child to tithe 10 percent of any money he receives from odd jobs or his birthday. Explain that the more we thank and honor God with giving, even when it's hard, the more delighted God is with our generosity!

More Americans claim to tithe than actually do: 17% of adults claim to tithe; 6% actually do so.

(Barna Group, 2000)

Money provides choices.

From being in control of your income to deciding how and why you'll spend money or when and if you fall into debt, money creates many choices in your life. And the decisions you make will ultimately affect everyone in your family—for better or for worse!

Good steward or spendthrift?

Are you frugal and thrifty with your money, often finding it hard to part with, or are you someone who lets money slip a little too easily through his fingers? Some people look for ways to save money by buying only when items are on sale. Others shop only to meet the needs of their families. Still

key point
WE CHOOSE HOW MONEY WILL BE USED.

others *love* spending and often find their credit cards with high balances. How we choose to use our money affects everything from how we sleep to what we eat! Being good stewards of our money means wise spending and saving. But being a spendthrift can mean worry, waste, and a lot of sleepless nights!

key point
BEING GOOD STEWARDS IS OFTEN HARD.

Children also fall into these same categories when it comes to managing their money. Have you ever seen how two kids with $5 each spend the money in different ways? One child may save it all and feel pride to know his piggy bank is full, while the other child may spend for toys and candy so that the money disappears in a snap!

INVITE YOUR CHILD TO TAKE THE FOLLOWING TRUE OR FALSE QUIZ WITH YOU, THEN SCORE YOUR ANSWERS.

1. You live for payday or allowance day!
2. You often dream about what you want to buy.
3. You can't seem to make money last for long.
4. You rarely have money left to save or donate.
5. You don't keep track of your spending or have a budget.
6. Having a lot of money makes you feel good inside.
7. You rarely buy things for others.
8. Money seems to control what you do each day.

Score your quiz as follows: Under three true answers, you're controlling your spending. If you had more than four true answers, you're a spendthrift who might be facing debt in the future, but you're not alone. Around 75 percent of Americans have been or will be in financial crisis at some point in their lives. Tell your child it's key to have control over her money and spending.

Give your child an assortment of coupons. Add up all of the savings from the coupons, then choose what you could do with the extra money. Remind your child that being a good steward means getting the most from his money!

TARGET MOMENT

Play a quick game of Save or Spend. Name pairs of items such as a boat and a bike. Then let your child tell which she would buy—or if she would rather save her money instead. Explain your choices. Encourage your child to think of long-range consequences of too many purchases and not enough savings!

God desires us to be good stewards who meet our needs, save some, and give a portion to Him. It takes responsibility, self-control, and wise decisions to be a good steward. If we choose to waste money, we can't meet our responsibilities—and we become poor stewards before God!

What we choose to do with our money can cost a lot!

Whatever we choose or choose not to do with our resources can either bring us financial success or financial failure down the road. Your child needs to realize that our choices surrounding money management affect us today *and* tomorrow!

If we overspend on items we truly don't need, there may be a shortage of cash that leaves us unable to meet daily obligations. For example, if you spent your child's lunch money on a new briefcase yesterday, he might go hungry at lunch today! Even though poor money decisions may not be felt immediately, they catch up to us in the future—and cost a great deal!

DON'T FORGET

Don't serve money;
let money
serve you!

PARENTS POINTER

Financial success doesn't just happen. It comes from a lot of hard work and good decisions regarding your money management. That's why modeling responsible spending and teaching your kids that money is not to be worshiped will help them make good money choices later in life.

key point
TODAY'S CHOICES AFFECT TOMORROW!

key point
CHOOSE TO USE MONEY WISELY!

Ask your child to think for a moment about the future and where he sees himself. Does he live in a nice house with a racy car parked outside? Now ask your child if he could afford his dreams on $50 or $100. Remind your child that without good choices to plan and save for the future, no one

BIG BIBLE POINT

Read I Timothy 6:10 with your child. Then discuss the following questions about choices and choosing not to love or worship money.

- What does this verse warn us about?
- How do poor money choices hurt us?
- What are good choices you can make about using money?

What determines our money decisions? If it's love of money and not caring about being a careful steward with resources, then money becomes our god. Most kids believe that having more money will solve any problem, but in fact, it can create even more! Remember: God tells us we cannot serve two masters—and choices must be made.

Place your spare change in a bowl. Then take turns naming things we may waste money on as you remove a coin from the bowl. After the coins are gone, point out that being broke is often a choice we make. Name good things that happen when we use money wisely as you deposit coins back into the bowl.

TREAT MONEY WITH RESPECT AND MAKE CHOICES WITH WISDOM.

How We Save Money

Whether you put your money in a traditional bank, in certificates of deposit, in a savings and loans, or even a piggy bank, you should see your savings grow given a little time, a bit of patience, and regularity with your deposits. Money that grows is money at work for us today—and tomorrow!

Saving is a virtue.

We strive to teach our children that patience is a virtue—a quality that's good to nurture in our lives and will help us live more fully. Saving money is also a virtue that, just like patience, helps us live more fully and securely!

Saving money calls for planning.

Saving is the cornerstone for accomplishing financial goals, providing emergency funds, and securing your future. A good savings plan requires regular contributions or deposits.

Your child will enjoy seeing how money that earns interest grows. Show him the chart indicating how putting $1,000 in an interest-paying savings account can grow to nearly $11,000 in thirty years.

IF YOU SAVED $1,000 YOUR MONEY WOULD GROW OVER THE YEARS! IT WOULD GROW EVEN MORE BY SAVING EACH MONTH!		
Years of saving	$1,000	Adding $100 every month
1	$1,083	$2,336
5	$1,490	$8,887
10	$2,220	$20,636
30	$10,936	$160,965

key point
SAVE REGULARLY.

Your child can use her allowance budget to plan how much and how often she can save—then encourage her to stick to her savings plan like glue! A good rule to remember is that it's not always how much you save to begin with but how often you save!

Encourage your child to create a savings plan for something he wants, such as a new video game. Then guide your child in putting his savings plan on paper. You could even add a picture of the desired item. Hang the plan where he will have a daily reminder of his goal and praise his efforts to save. Remind your child that planning and saving help us reach our goals!

key point
STICK TO YOUR SAVINGS PLAN!

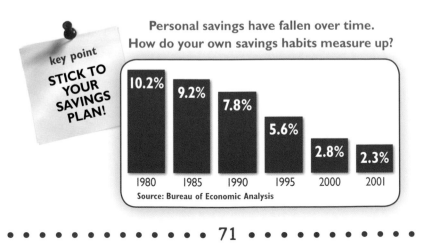

Personal savings have fallen over time. How do your own savings habits measure up?

10.2% — 1980
9.2% — 1985
7.8% — 1990
5.6% — 1995
2.8% — 2000
2.3% — 2001

Source: Bureau of Economic Analysis

Saving money requires patience.

Good things come to those who wait. You've heard this saying from your parents, teachers, or even your spouse over the course of your life, and you've probably shared it with your kids! But patience can be hard for kids, who are experts of impatience and instant gratification! Kids would love to see their money grow quickly, but unfortunately, most don't have a lot of money in their savings accounts. Their money will grow with time and interest, but it takes patience, too.

Patience in saving money is not unlike learning to ride a bike. It was only after practice, time, patience—and a few spills—that your child was able to ride like the wind! Saving money requires practice by contributing regularly; it requires time for money to add up over months or years; and it takes patience to wait for interest to multiply your money.

"The key to everything is patience. You get the chicken by hatching the egg, not by smashing it open."

—Arnold H. Glasgow

BIG BIBLE POINT

Remember how God blessed and rewarded Abram's patience and obedience with a baby and great wealth? Remind your child of the value of patience and how God helps us wait for the blessings He will send!

key point
GOOD THINGS COME TO THOSE WHO WAIT.

There's an African folktale about a man and woman who wanted a baby very much. The man crossed a river to ask God for a baby and was told that, when he returned, the couple would receive a baby, patience, and wealth—but only one could be kept. When the three gifts arrived, the wise couple decided patience would serve them best. But as the baby and money sadly left, they realized it would take great patience to cross the river. so they returned to the couple, who now had a baby, patience, and wealth!

> Patience can be a challenging quality for young kids to nurture in their lives, especially when it comes to saving money. Be realistic and try not to set too-far distant savings goals when your child is young.

Help your child understand how patience works to multiply money. Invite your child to drop grains of rice, one by one, into a bowl. With time and patience there is soon a bowl full of rice! Point out that time, patience, and regular saving increases the money we have.

key point

SAVING TAKES TIME TO ADD UP.

TIPS FOR TODDLERS

Encourage your toddler to save and have patience all at one time! Draw a simple bunch of balloons, gumballs, or coins by a piggy bank. Each time your child saves a few coins in her bank, have her color in the same number of shapes. As her savings grow, so do her patience and lovely pictures! Collect them in a book to enjoy over and over.

Impatience is a 'tween's middle name. Remind her it takes time to build dreams!

Safely set aside your money.

It's important to set aside your money, but it's equally important to make sure your money is safe! Whether you invest your money or put it in an account at a bank, keeping your money safe keeps you at peace and helps you feel secure.

Banks are safe places to save.

Everyone loves piggy banks, and they're a great way for kids to begin saving their money. The upside to piggy banks? They're handy—no driving through narrow drive-up windows. They're portable and travel with you when you move. And they're irresistibly cute! But let's face it, piggy banks

INTERESTING ...

BUT NO INTEREST!

are much too easy to withdraw from and aren't the safest—or most profitable—places to trust your savings to!

key point
BANK INTEREST HELPS MONEY GROW.

Traditional banks and savings and loans are usually safe places in which to keep money. Both pay interest on balances on money deposited into passbook accounts, and both are insured. Explain to your child that if money was kept in a piggy bank and there was a fire or theft, the money would be gone. Remind your child that managing money requires careful thought and good decisions—and keeping money in a savings account in a bank can be a wise choice.

key point
BANKS ARE SAFE AND INSURED.

Remind your child of the parable of the Talents and how one man hid his money in a field. After many months the money was dug up. Was there more than when he first buried it? Nope—his money didn't grow! This is like keeping money in a piggy bank, a sock, or a box. If we want our money to grow, then a bank is one place that pays interest on the money. Point out that when we're good stewards of our money, we keep it safe and growing!

Read the parable of the Lost Coin to your child from Luke 15:8, 9. Ask how keeping money safe shows good stewardship.

TIPS FOR TODDLERS
Let your toddler put loose change through the slot in a piggy bank. (Watch that coins go in the bank and not the mouth!) This helps his eye-hand coordination while having fun with saving money!

You can use both a piggy bank and a traditional bank. First encourage your child to fill his piggy bank with allowance money or loose coins he finds. Once the bank is full, you can separate the coins into piles of pennies, nickels, dimes, and quarters. Purchase coin sleeves from a hobby store or the bank, then let your child make his own coin rolls. Your child will feel proud as he deposits the money into his account at the bank.

Go on a tour of a bank vault. Inquire at your bank or savings and loan to see if you and your child can visit the vault. Encourage your child to ask questions about how safe money really is in a bank and what kind of natural disasters a bank vault can withstand. You might be surprised how safe a "safe" really is!

Investing money can be a wise choice.

Investing money means placing it where it can grow. Some people buy savings bonds from the government or a public utilities company. These companies pay you for "renting" or using your money for a certain length of time, and you end up having more money than you originally invested.

key point
INVEST WISELY AND SAFELY!

key point
INVESTMENTS INCLUDE STOCKS AND BONDS.

TIPS FOR 'TWEENS
Have your older child look in the paper daily for what a specific stock is doing. It could be the company that makes her favorite toy, cereal, or soda. Track it on a piece of paper for a week or month and graph the results. Would that company be a good investment?

Kids hear a lot about stocks and the stock market in today's economy. Explain that stocks are small portions of a larger company. Companies sell stocks to help them grow. When stocks go up, your investment goes up, too. But if stock prices fall, you lose money. Investing through stocks can be a bit risky, so it's good to make careful choices about where to put your money!

Kids are like sponges and pick up on your enthusiasm! Get them excited about investing early on to help them make wise choices in the future.

There are many considerations when investing your money. Kids need to understand that first you need a good idea of how much money you can invest and how much you can afford to lose—if any. Investing in the stock market can be risky, with no guarantees you'll make more money than you started with. But when you do make money, it is usually more than what you would make at a bank. You need to set savings goals that are realistic and understand that whether you're saving in a bank, through investing in bonds, or through the stock market, it takes time, careful thought, and patience to invest!

CONSIDER THIS ...

- **What are my investing habits?**
- **Do I have patience with my investments?**
- **Are my expectations of return realistic?**
- **Have I put all my eggs in one basket?**
- **How can wise investments help my child?**

TARGET MOMENT

For a small amount of money, your child can purchase a U.S. Savings Bond. Explain that the bond will be worth even more money in the future. Keep the bond in a safe place where your child can see it often as a reminder of making wise investments with his money.

No human can predict the future; only God has the power to know what is ahead of us. But God provides us with the ability to make good decisions and to be prepared. Your older child would enjoy a trip to an investment firm to learn more about stocks and bonds. Help him write a list of questions such as "Who should invest money?" and "What kinds of stocks do people buy?" There are many places to invest your money—but one thing is sure: Investing safely and wisely can pay big dividends!

Investing requires time, patience, and consistency!

Saving money secures our futures.

Saving for "rainy days" or to secure your future requires careful planning. Security doesn't just happen—it takes solid saving over the years.

Save for "rainy days."

In Aesop's Fable "The Ant and the Grasshopper," Grasshopper is content to use his sunny summer days singing, hopping, and not caring about tomorrow. As Grasshopper played, Ant worked to store up grain and other foods for winter. When winter days came, who was prepared for the tough times? The ant, of course! And too late Grasshopper learned the importance of preparing for rainy—or snowy—days!

Kids are eternal optimists, and the future is so very far ahead of them that it only exists in a kind of "someday fairyland." But the future is real and will come. And along with those future days will come unforeseen emergencies and those proverbial rainy days!

BIG BIBLE POINT

Think for a moment about Noah and the planning it took for his rainy days! Tell your child that Noah was to save up food for his family and all the animals on the ark to last them through their rainy days. Ask your child why this was important and what might have happened if Noah had not saved for a rainy day.

key point
"RAINY DAYS" COME TO EVERYONE.

Kids have rainy days, although they may consist of blown bike tires or broken windows that must be repaired. Discuss with your child how money can help for unplanned repairs or emergencies. Ask what would happen if there were not enough money to cover these expenses and how saving money now can help in the future.

key point
MONEY HELPS WITH EMERGENCIES!

The fable "The Ant and the Grasshopper" has a biblical basis. Read aloud Proverbs 30:25 and 13:11. Compare what the Bible teaches us about saving for a rainy day and what the fable teaches. Then have your child name three good reasons to begin saving today for unplanned events tomorrow.

Let your child illustrate a scene from the story of the Ant and the Grasshopper on a sheet of paper. Discuss how Grasshopper's lack of planning or saving food is like people not saving money for rainy days. Have your child explain if he's more an "ant" or a "grasshopper" and why. Then write "Save for rainy days!" across the top of the illustration. Encourage your child to hang the picture as a reminder that tomorrow will come—and we want to be ready!

TIPS FOR 'TWEENS

Have your child save some money for the next rainy day—literally! Encourage your child to save a bit of money back for something fun to do on the next rainy day. Maybe he will buy a new computer game or video. Remind your child that rainy days happen to everyone and that saving for unplanned emergencies is wise!

Save for security.

The state of being safe and not in danger is what the word "security" means. Most people would probably say they have only a partial feeling of financial security. So how can you put your child on the road to financial security early? By careful spending and sound saving!

TARGET MOMENT

Balance your child's feelings of what constitutes security by pointing out that money can help us feel secure from unplanned expenses but that it isn't the only thing that offers security. Loving parents and caregivers, teachers, and church leaders all offer security today—and of course God and His powerful Word offer us security and safety all the time!

key point
REGULAR SAVING STRENGTHENS SECURITY.

key point
THE FUTURE IS COMING!

BIG BIBLE POINT

Read Ecclesiastes 7:12 aloud with your child, then discuss the following questions:

• Why is wisdom important when saving money?

• Would you rather have wisdom or money? Explain.

• How can wisdom also bring us money?

• Is it wise or foolish to save money for the future? Explain.

In order to achieve financial security, we must acquire skills, knowledge, and the motivation to make good choices—even when they're hard. Stopping yourself from buying a new "whim" may feel disappointing, but consistent savings and wise investing will help you achieve security for the future—our whims will not!

Each time you make a deposit in your savings or retirement account, say, "Saving today for tomorrow makes great sense!" Repeating a short catch phrase to your kids helps them equate saving money with being a smart thing to do. After a time, don't be surprised if your kids are repeating your own wise words!

Help your child understand what "security" means by asking her what makes her feel comfortable and safe. Is it a certain blanket or having loving parents and a safe home to live in? Whatever makes her feel safe gives her a sense of security. Ask your child what it would be like to lose that security. Explain that these are the same feelings we'd have if our money were gone.

When you get into the car, ask your child if he would feel secure without a seatbelt. Discuss the importance of wearing a seatbelt all the time to feel secure and not only wearing it once in a while. Explain that if we saved for the future only once in a while, we wouldn't be protected either. Regular savings protects us from emergencies and gives us security for the future.

What makes us feel financially insecure?

- Too much unnecessary spending
- Too much credit-card debt
- Too expensive car loans
- Too high of mortgage loans
- Student loans
- Poor financial planning
- Too little regular savings

Save for future needs.

Do you think about retirement and what you will need once you're no longer working? Your needs change as you grow older. Will you travel in retirement, or will you have a second home in Arizona? You probably have visions of what life will be like in your golden years, but are you doing all that you can now to accomplish your goals for tomorrow? And how can you help your child understand the importance of planning for his own future needs?

key point
SAVING REQUIRES TIME.

Since kids aren't even of working age yet, they have a difficult time understanding that stopping regular work because of age means less money and more medical expenses! Help your child understand changing needs by asking if he could wear the same clothes he has on now in ten or twenty years and why not. Point out that his clothes fit fine today, but as he gets older, his needs for certain things will change. If money hasn't been set aside for new clothes, your child would be wearing some frightfully outgrown jeans!

key point
INVEST IN YOUR FUTURE!

Cut a large cloud shape from white poster board. Tell your child this cloud represents "someday" and the things he might like to do. Challenge him to draw, list, or glue magazine pictures to the cloud to show what he'd like his future to hold. Remind your child that everything is possible—with time, patience, and regular savings!

"Our future will not be determined by chance, but rather by the choices we make today."
—Bill Richardson

Explain that as we grow older, our needs never stop changing and the money we save helps us provide for changing needs. Retirement means a loss of regular income for most people, while health-care concerns and expenses usually increase. If we haven't saved enough, it may be hard to provide medical care as well as housing, food, and clothing.

Social Security checks from the government are one way people receive money when they no longer work regular jobs. But most people need more money to live. Help your child realize that the extra funds must come from the money we've saved. If we're careful about saving money all our lives, we'll have our needs met—and many of our wants as well!

TRY THIS!

Share the chart below with your child and ask him how the needs kids have today might change as they grow older and why. Encourage your child to tell you if his needs are much the same as the ones listed, how he thinks his own needs and wants will change in the future, and what he can do to plan for meeting those needs.

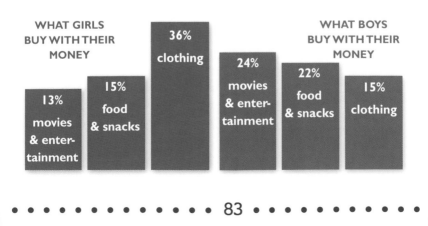

WHAT GIRLS BUY WITH THEIR MONEY

13% movies & entertainment

15% food & snacks

36% clothing

WHAT BOYS BUY WITH THEIR MONEY

24% movies & entertainment

22% food & snacks

15% clothing

We save to accomplish our goals.

Saving money allows you to accomplish your goals, no matter how large or how small. Only you set your short- and long-term goals, and only you can prepare to achieve them!

Money provides for the short term.

Short-term savings goals allow you to save for items that don't cost much or that you plan to purchase in the near future. Short-term goals might include saving for "today" spending: lunch with a friend or even a special birthday gift. Other goals require a longer time to save and might include saving for a new appliance or for a summer vacation.

key point
IDENTIFY SHORT-TERM GOALS.

Ask your child to identify some of her own short-term needs and wants. Guide your child to name ways her goals can be met, such as through hard work, saving money, and curbing other spending. Are her goals worth the work? True goals are the ones we are willing to work hard at achieving—otherwise they may just be frivolous wants and not true needs!

DON'T FORGET

Short-term goals are often overlooked for bigger goals. If your child is only setting his heart on a large, long-range goal, encourage him to set a series of smaller, more reachable goals as he works his way toward "the big one"!

key point
MAKE A PLAN TO ACHIEVE YOUR GOALS.

Since most short-term goals are relatively easy to reach, adults won't have much trouble attaining them. But kids have to work hard in order to reach even their short-term goals. Saving to buy what we want with our own money feels good, and by putting money aside regularly, short-term goals can be achieved. Assure your child she can do it with patience and perseverance.

CONSIDER THIS ...

- *What are your own short-term goals?*
- *How does setting goals affect your life?*
- *In what ways is it good to model goal-setting?*
- *In what ways is it good to model goal-getting?*

"Of what use is money in the hand of a fool, since he has no desire to get wisdom?" (Proverbs 17:16)

- *How does this relate to some-one who just wants to spend and not save his money?*
- *What can you do to make sure you are not a "fool" with your money?*

Challenge your child to identify one short-term goal he has, such as buying a ticket to a theme park or purchasing a digital camera. Determine how much savings the goal requires, then help your child form a plan to achieve his goal. Your plan may include making a special bank in which to save for his goal. Remember that a parent's encouragement for short-term goals can really help in the long term!

Money provides for the long term.

Short-term goals are easier and usually quicker to save for, but it's long-term goals that may be more fulfilling once you achieve them. Long-term savings goals are goals in which you save for items that require larger amounts of money and take much longer to save for. These items can include anything for "tomorrow spending" or for securing your future. Saving for your child's college tuition, for a nice down payment on a brand new home, or a retirement trip around the world are considered long-term goals.

key point
LONG-TERM GOALS TAKE LONG-TERM SAVING.

Long-term saving for "tomorrow" spending requires commitment, time, and patience. Explain to your child that long-term goals are ones that reach into the future and require diligent and consistent savings to achieve. Let your child name some long-term goals your family might have plus a few for himself. Most long-range goals remain constant by the time a child reaches adulthood.

IF YOU COULD SAVE $100 PER MONTH, JUST LOOK AT YOUR LONG-TERM SAVINGS!

Annual Percentage Rate	In 10 Years	In 15 Years	In 20 Years	In 25 Years	In 30 Years
8.0	$18,120.59	$34,215.46	$58,131.59	$93,669.69	$146,477.45
9.0	$19,135.85	$37,335.13	$65,737.27	$110,053.95	$179,213.66
10.0	$20,220.77	$40,797.48	$74,514.81	$129,964.60	$220,297.80

*compounded quarterly

Whereas short-term goals can be met by putting money in a regular savings account, long-term goals require long-term investments in banks, mutual funds, money-market accounts, bonds, certificates of deposit, or even stocks. A good rule of thumb for your child to remember is that long-term goals require long-term savings!

key point
LONG-TERM SAVING REQUIRES COMMITMENT!

It's wise to teach your child that it's never too early to start saving for something really big—even if he may not know what that "something" is yet! Don't expect too much from your child in the way of saving for long-term goals today; most kids can't fathom going to school for years after high school! Realize that your child is probably most interested in his own short-term goals and that long-term goals may be too ethereal for him to imagine right now.

FINISHING SCHOOL MAY BE ONE GOAL YOUR CHILD HAS, BUT IT'S ONLY THE BEGINNING!

TIPS FOR TODDLERS

Help your toddler understand the difference between something taking a short time and something requiring a longer time. Draw a small apple and a large apple. Let your toddler color the apples, pointing out that the larger one takes longer to color while the smaller one takes a shorter amount of time.

Merely realizing that some goals are longer away and require long-term planning and saving is probably enough for now. Remind your child that all goals—large and small—need thought, careful decisions, and some form of regular and consistent savings plan to be achieved!

Money can grow in many ways.

You may never be a millionaire, but you must invest and save in order to be comfortable for the future—and for today!

Lost time is lost money.

Procrastination is one of our worst enemies, and it is no respecter of age. Kids as well as grown-ups tend to put things off and adopt wait-and-see attitudes. Procrastinating about mowing the lawn creates a field we may need to mow twice. Ask your child to name other ways procrastinating affects our lives.

If procrastination affects our front lawns, imagine what it does to saving money! When we start saving early and often, our money builds at a faster rate. Your child can understand that if he begins collecting stamps when he's ten, he will have a lot of stamps and a super collection by the time he's eighty years old! But if he doesn't begin to collect those stamps until he is seventy-five, there's not much time to collect those stamps.

TARGET MOMENT

Benjamin Franklin wrote, "You may delay, but time will not." Discuss with your child how this saying relates to saving money and what happens when we delay or don't save money for the future.

key point
WAITING CAN COST PLENTY!

key point
SAVE MONEY STARTING NOW!

Look at the Power of Procrastination chart. It is surprising to realize that someone who saved for six years had more money than someone who put off saving for six years but invested $2,000 a year for the next 37 years! Help your child see what putting off saving his money can do. It's one of the best lessons you can teach him about money!

Helping your child learn about the negative power of procrastination early will help him make better choices in the future. This goes not only for getting papers signed but also for saving and investing money. Help your child understand that lost time is lost money!

THE POWER OF PROCRASTINATION

Person A			Person B		
Age	Payment	Accumulation End of Year	Age	Payment	Accumulation End of Year
22	$2,000	$2,254	22	$0	$0
23	$2,000	$4,793	23	$0	$0
24	$2,000	$7,655	24	$0	$0
25	$2,000	$10,879	25	$0	$0
26	$2,000	$14,513	26	$0	$0
27	$2,000	$18,607	27	$0	$0
28	$0	$20,967	28	$2,000	$2,254
29	$0	$23,626	29	$2,000	$4,793
30	$0	$24,622	30	$2,000	$7,655
31	$0	$29,999	31	$2,000	$10,879
32	$0	$33,803	32	$2,000	$14,513
37	$0	$61,410	37	$2,000	$40,877
42	$0	$111,563	42	$2,000	$88,774
47	$0	$202,676	47	$2,000	$175,788
52	$0	$368,200	52	$2,000	$333,867
57	$0	$668,907	57	$2,000	$621,048
62	$0	$1,215,202	62	$2,000	$1,142,768
65	$0	$1,738,673	65	$2,000	$1,640,437

* based on a 12% IRA

Even millionaires save!

Who would think that millionaires save their money? Kids especially tend to see millionaires as having so much to spend and enjoy that they'd never be bothered with saving money—only spending it. From yachts and jewels to private jets and jaunts around the world, kids envy millionaires for their freedom of spending. But if you remind your child that millionaires saved their money to become millionaires, she will realize that even the richest of the people in the world save their money, too.

Although millionaires are able to afford luxury cars, gold watches, flashy clothes, mansions, and more, many millionaires live relatively simple lives. Many are found to have the least expensive long-distance phone carriers and are frugal with utilities, foods, and everyday items. The point is, most millionaires have worked hard for their money! They worked hard to get it, and they work hard to make it grow—just as we try to do with our own money.

TIPS FOR 'TWEENS
How long does it take to count to a million? You can try counting one by one (which would take days), figure out a mathematical equation, or skip-count. Remind your 'tween that just as counting to a million takes a while, saving money to reach a million requires time and patience as well!

✓ Money is nice, but remember: "It is the heart that makes a man rich. He is rich according to what he is, not according to what he has."
—Henry Ward Beecher

You too can work toward becoming a millionaire, but you must meet your needs and watch your spending on unnecessary items. You must save and invest money and be patient while doing all of these things. Remind your child that money is easier to make than it is to hold on to but that we have the power, just as millionaires do, to save our money and put it to work for us.

If you placed $1 bills end to end, they would travel about 100 miles to make a **MILLION DOLLARS!**

Kids have a hard time understanding just how much one million is. They know it's a lot of money, but how can you help your child comprehend how much makes one million? Tell your child that the largest bill in circulation is the $100 bill. It would take 10,000 of those bills to make one million dollars. This stack of money would make a stack of $100 bills about 3½ feet tall! Would he like to have this amount of money? You bet he would, and now would be a great time for him to start saving!

TARGET MOMENT

Discuss what this awesome equation means and how it relates to achieving financial hopes and dreams: "Conceive + Believe = Achieve" (Denis Waitley).

key point
MILLIONAIRES SAVE AND INVEST.

key point
BEING RICH IS POSSIBLE!

More Resources

BOOKS

for kids

- Judith Viorst, *Alexander, Who Used to be Rich Last Sunday* (Aladdin, 1987).
- Stan and Jan Berenstain, *The Berenstain Bears' Dollars and Sense* (Random House, 2001).
- Stan and Jan Berenstain, *The Berenstain Bears' Trouble with Money* (Random House, 1983).
- Barbara Johnston Adams, *The Go-Around Dollar* (Simon & Schuster, 1992).
- Heather Wood, 101 *Marvelous Money-Making Ideas for Kids* (Tor Books, 1995).
- Gail Karlitz and Debbie Honig, *Growing Money—A Complete (and Completely Updated!) Investing Guide for Kids* (Price Stern Sloan, 2001).

for parents

- Paul W. Lermitte, *Making Allowances: A Dollars-And-Sense Guide to Teaching Kids About Money* (McGraw-Hill, 2002).
- Pat Smith and Lynn Roney, *Wow the Dow! The Complete Guide to Teaching Your Kids How to Invest in the Stock Market* (Fireside, 2000).
- Jayne A. Pearl, *Kids and Money: Giving Them Savvy to Succeed Financially* (Bloomberg Press, 1999).
- Larry Burkett, *Your Child and Money: A Family Activity Book* (Moody Press, 2000).
- Larry Burkett and Rick Osborne, *Financial Parenting* (Moody Press, 1999).

WEB SITES

- www.kidsmoney.org
- www.kidsbank.com
- www.kidsturncentral.com/links/moneylinks.htm
- www.keepkidshealthy.com/interest_your_kids_in/kids_money.html
- www.kids.gov/k_money.htm
- www.ustreas.gov

GAMES AND TOYS

- Large Money Savvy Piggy Bank (Money Savvy Generation). A four-chambered piggy bank that gives children money choices when they receive money: save, spend, donate, or invest; ages 4-11.
- Wall Street Spin (Fun Spin). Pretend you're a Wall Street Tycoon while working on math skills; ages 10+.
- You're Bluffing Card Game (Ravensburger). Use money cards to bluff and win animal sets of four with the highest value. Then auction off cards to the highest bidder; ages 7+.
- YOUniverse Amazing Money Jar (Summit Products). Cool ATM to keep track of deposits and withdrawals; ages 5+.
- MoneyWise Kids (Aristoplay). Two fast-paced games that improve making change and budgeting skills; ages 7-11.

Subpoint Index

Chapter 3: How We Use Money   48

Chapter 4: How We Save Money   70